Who Is Beyoncé?

by Kirsti Jewel

illustrated by Dede Putra

Penguin Workshop

For Samara, Katie, and Leslie—for the many hours
we pretended we were Destiny's Child—KJ

PENGUIN WORKSHOP
An imprint of Penguin Random House LLC
1745 Broadway, New York, New York 10019

First published in the United States of America by Penguin Workshop,
an imprint of Penguin Random House LLC, 2025

Visit us online at penguinrandomhouse.com.

Library of Congress Cataloging-in-Publication Data is available.

Printed in the United States of America

ISBN 9798217049318 (paperback)   10 9 8 7 6 5 4 3 2 1 CJKW
ISBN 9798217049325 (library binding)   10 9 8 7 6 5 4 3 2 1 CJKW

The authorized representative in the EU for product safety and compliance is
Penguin Random House Ireland, Morrison Chambers, 32 Nassau Street,
Dublin D02 YH68, Ireland, https://eu-contact.penguin.ie.

Contents

Who Is Beyoncé?

More than one hundred thousand people crowd around a stage in the middle of a California desert on April 14, 2018. They have been waiting almost a year for this moment.

A woman dressed in a honey-colored marching band uniform starts the show by playing a single drum. The crowd roars. "Beychella"—part of the Coachella music festival—is finally beginning.

As the drumming continues, men holding black banners step aside, one by one. Behind them, there are several majorettes—dancers who accompany a marching band. Finally, they present Beyoncé. She's dressed in a drum major costume. Her black, gold, and silver bodysuit glimmers. It's draped by a black cape with a gold-and-silver lining that glitters. An image of an ancient Egyptian queen is on the back of her cape. Beyoncé is wearing a towering crown of her own.

She struts down a runway. Her dancers follow behind her. Once they get to the main stage, the majorettes continue dancing. Their captain, Beyoncé, has disappeared, and they must keep the attention of the thousands of fans.

Behind the dancers are rows and rows of mostly Black musicians. Beyoncé has brought hundreds onto this historic stage with her: a marching band, violin players, baton twirlers, and more.

The beloved musician returns to the stage in a new costume and sings her heart out. She's waited a year for this moment after having to postpone

her performance while she was pregnant. Now, she is back and filled with joy. The stage is her second home. This is her homecoming.

CHAPTER 1
Growing Up Country

Beyoncé Giselle Knowles was born on September 4, 1981, in Houston, Texas. Her mother, Tina, was a hairdresser. Her father, Mathew, worked in sales at a big company called Xerox. When Beyoncé was almost five years old, her sister, Solange, was born.

Beyoncé grew up listening to all kinds of music. Motown and R&B played in the Knowles home. Being a girl from Texas, Beyoncé also loved country songs. Every year, her family would go to the Houston Livestock Show and Rodeo. They would dress in their finest cowboy outfits and watch the cowboys and cowgirls do tricks on their horses. But her southern roots didn't stop there. Beyoncé was raised with influences from her parents' southern upbringings.

Her mother is from Louisiana and her father is from Alabama. Every summer, Beyoncé and her sister would visit her grandparents in Alabama, where her grandfather would sing them to sleep with country music.

When Beyoncé was a little girl, she was very shy. She kept to herself and didn't have many friends. This worried her parents, so they decided to enroll Beyoncé in dance lessons. They hoped she would make friends.

It was through the teachings of the dance studio owner, Ms. Johnson, that Beyoncé discovered her gift of dance. When the class learned a routine, Beyoncé perfected every move. And she wouldn't hold anything back!

"Beyoncé would dance so hard that she would lose her costume pieces. Sometimes her hat would come off because she was fierce," Ms. Johnson once said.

Dance wasn't the only gift discovered during dance class. One day, Ms. Johnson was teaching her class and started to sing the dance's song. Suddenly, she heard someone else singing beautifully. It was Beyoncé!

When Beyoncé's talents were discovered, her parents encouraged her. Once they took her to see a Michael Jackson concert. After the impressive show, Beyoncé knew she wanted to perform, too. When she was seven, she entered her first talent show. She sang "Imagine" by John Lennon. Once Beyoncé got onstage, it was like she was at Ms. Johnson's studio again. She was confident and joyful.

As Beyoncé got older, her love for performing increased. In 1990, she joined a group called Girl's Tyme. The group had three singers and three dancers. Beyoncé was one of the singers.

Girl's Tyme

The group performed all over Houston and became popular. They even performed on *Star Search*, the most popular talent show on TV at the time! The girls practiced hard. Their excellent routine included singing, dancing, and rapping. They lost, but a manager from the show saw their talent. He told Mathew that Girl's Tyme was great, but they needed more practice. So, that's what they did—practice, practice, practice.

CHAPTER 2
Destiny's Child

Gradually, Girl's Tyme got better. The group performed around Houston and became local celebrities. In between church and school, Girl's Tyme practiced at the Knowleses' house. They even practiced at Tina's hair salon.

As Tina's clients got their hair styled, the girls danced, rapped, and sang for them. After their performances, Tina's clients would give feedback on how the girls could improve. When they were lucky, customers would tip the girls for their performance. Beyoncé also earned money from sweeping the floors. She used her tip money to buy a season pass to Six Flags, an amusement park.

Between rehearsals and booking more shows, it soon became clear that Girl's Tyme needed a full-time manager. So, Mathew quit his well-paying job and stepped into that role. Eventually, Tina left the salon to focus on supporting the girls, too. She did their hair and sewed their outfits. Quitting their jobs to support Beyoncé wasn't easy. The family had to sell their big house and move to a smaller apartment, but they believed their efforts would be worth it.

In 1996, Mathew secured a deal with

Columbia Records. By now, Girl's Tyme had changed their name to Destiny's Child. There were now four members from Girl's Tyme— Beyoncé, LeToya Luckett, LaTavia Roberson, and Kelly Rowland.

LaTavia, Kelly, Beyoncé, and LeToya

Destiny's Child recorded a few songs in major studios, but their first big success was a song called "No, No, No." The song was released in 1997 and was on their debut album, *Destiny's Child.*

After the success of their first album, Destiny's Child recorded the album that made them a household name—*The Writing's on the Wall*. They worked  with big-time producers and songwriters. Some of its most successful songs were cowritten by Kandi Burruss, from the popular girl group Xscape. She was known for writing catchy songs that empower women, a message that was important to Destiny's Child. One of the songs she wrote was "Bills, Bills, Bills." It was nominated for many awards.

The huge success of *The Writing's on the*  *Wall* brought wonderful opportunities. The group got to travel the world and meet celebrities they admired. Best of all, they got to perform!

But trouble soon came. LaTavia and LeToya felt like they weren't getting the attention they deserved from Mathew. They accused him of favoring Beyoncé and Kelly. They said he liked them more because they were his daughters. This was because Kelly had moved in with the Knowles family when she was a little girl when her family was going through difficult times. The Knowles family took care of Kelly and always called her their daughter. LaTavia and LeToya left the group.

Kelly Rowland

When the music video from "Say My Name" came out, LaTavia and LeToya were replaced by new members, Farrah Franklin and Michelle Williams. Soon, Farrah left the group, too.

These changes in the group were hard for

Farrah Franklin and Michelle Williams

Beyoncé. She didn't want people to feel left out. It was also difficult for her to read what other people were saying about her and the group. Lies and rumors were spread about Beyoncé and her family. During this time, she spent a lot of hours crying and found it difficult to get out of bed. Later, she said this was one of the most difficult times of her career. Her bond with Kelly and Michelle, however, proved to be solid. Forming Destiny's Child may have been difficult, but once Michelle was added to the group, it felt like Destiny's Child was always meant to be those three singers.

The trio recorded three more studio albums.

Their songs, which were major hits on both R&B and pop charts, inspired girls and women to be strong. "Independent Women Part 1," their number one song, and Destiny's Child became a symbol for women's empowerment and sisterhood.

CHAPTER 3
Beyoncé Goes Solo

At the age of nineteen, Beyoncé was doing what she loved. She was performing with her two best friends. With her dad as the manager and her mother as the stylist, she was able to travel the world with her family. Even her little sister, Solange, went on the road with the group.

As Beyoncé experienced success with Destiny's Child, she continued to expand her career. In 2002, she released a song called "'03 Bonnie & Clyde" with famous rapper Jay-Z. The two met in 2000 at a music festival. Shortly after meeting, there were whispers about them dating, but they both denied it. In the music video for the song, the two musicians played characters who were a couple, which led more people to believe the rumors.

That same year, Beyoncé started working on her first solo album. She was in the studio nonstop, working with musicians she admired like Missy Elliott, Luther Vandross, and Sean Paul. Just as she was ready to release the album, Beyoncé was asked to wait. Kelly had just released a song called "Dilemma" with rapper Nelly.

Solange

Solange Knowles is a singer, songwriter, and actress. Just like her sister, she began performing at a young age. She first performed when she was five years old at the Six Flags in Houston. She eventually became a backup dancer for Destiny's Child but always had her own goals. When she was fifteen, she recorded the theme song for a Disney Channel show called *The Proud Family*. Destiny's Child were her backup singers for the song.

Solange has been in several films and television shows. By 2024, she'd released four albums. Solange won a Grammy Award for her song "Cranes in the Sky," which was on her album *A Seat at the Table*. She's known for being a fashion icon and won a *Glamour* award for Woman of the Year.

The record label didn't want it to seem like two members of the biggest girl group were competing with each other. Beyoncé was disappointed, but she understood. She did not want to distract from her best friend's new song.

So, she waited. The extra time allowed her to work on her album even more. Just when Beyoncé thought she was done recording, she heard a new song—one that would change her career forever!

One day a producer named Rich Harrison said he had some new music that he thought would be perfect for Beyoncé. The two arranged a meeting in the studio. The sound was energetic and lively. It was a sample from a song from the 1970s called "Are You My Woman (Tell Me So)" by the Chi-Lites. As soon as Rich played

Rich Harrison

the music, Beyoncé loved it. The only problem was that there weren't any lyrics.

But Beyoncé was distracted. It was Kelly's birthday and she needed to buy her a present. She asked Rich to begin the lyrics to the song while she went to shop for Kelly. She promised to be back in two hours.

As she was getting ready to leave, she realized she didn't look as put together as she'd like. She knew if she left the studio, people would photograph her, and she couldn't be looking a mess! Her clothes were mismatched and her hair wasn't combed right. She told Rich, "I'm looking so crazy right now." When Beyoncé said this, Rich was inspired—he decided this could be the chorus for the song! "Crazy in Love" was born. It featured Jay-Z and was released in May 2003.

Beyoncé's first solo album, *Dangerously in Love*, was released the following month. She received many awards for the album, including five Grammy Awards. Between 2003 and 2004, "Crazy in Love" alone received over ten awards.

This would be the beginning of many more hits to come for Beyoncé.

In 2004, another debut took place. Beyoncé and Jay-Z attended the MTV Video Music Awards together. This was their first red carpet event as an official couple, and it was an exciting night. Now, the world knew they were dating. Jay took home four awards that evening, and Beyoncé won an award for Best Female Video for "Naughty Girl."

CHAPTER 4
Endings and Beginnings

On June 11, 2005, Beyoncé was emotional. She was where she felt most at home—onstage with her best friends, Kelly and Michelle.

Destiny's Child was in Barcelona, Spain, and they were in the final city of their European tour called Destiny Fulfilled . . . and Lovin' It. Their album *Destiny Fulfilled* was released the previous year and had a lot of success.

But since that release, the group hadn't had much time together. Each member was busy working on their own projects. Michelle had

released two albums. Kelly had released one solo album and was exploring acting. And Beyoncé was working on her second solo album, *B'Day*. She was also starring in two films: *The Pink Panther* and *Dreamgirls*.

Destiny's Child had an announcement to make. Kelly was given the task of sharing the decision that the women had made together: "We have been working together as Destiny's Child since we were nine, and touring together since we were fourteen," Kelly said. "After a lot of discussion and some deep soul searching, we realized that our current tour has given us the opportunity to leave Destiny's Child on a high note, united in our friendship and filled with an overwhelming gratitude for our music, our fans, and each other."

The fans found out Destiny's Child was ending. After the announcement, the group gave an interview. Beyoncé said that they were grateful for their success but most grateful to still be best friends.

Beyonce released *B'Day* on her twenty-fifth birthday. The album took just three weeks to record! Beyoncé worked with multiple producers so that the album had a unique, varied sound. Beyoncé also worked alongside Solange. Her sister cowrote two of the songs on the album—"Get Me Bodied" and "Upgrade U"—and the track "Flaws and All" on the deluxe edition. The first single, "Deja Vu" (which featured Jay-Z), was very

popular. *B'Day* was nominated for five Grammy Awards and won the award for Best Contemporary R&B Album.

On April 4, 2008, a special delivery arrived for Beyoncé in New York City—seventy thousand white orchids! They were a surprise on a very special day—her wedding day!

The date is special because it highlights Beyoncé and Jay-Z's shared love for the number four. Beyoncé's birthday is September 4, and Jay-Z's birthday is December 4. They even have matching number four tattoos on their ring fingers.

Beyoncé wore a simple white dress made by her mother. The wedding was small with only forty guests. Everyone was asked to keep their phones outside to make sure the wedding was private.

In October, Beyoncé officially shared that she and Jay-Z were married. She shared the news through an article in *Essence* magazine.

"Single Ladies (Put a Ring on It)" was released that fall and the rest of her album *I Am . . . Sasha Fierce* was released in November.

The album had eight slower songs, such as "If I Were a Boy" and the popular song "Halo." It also had eight upbeat songs, including "Diva." Featuring two different styles of music was on purpose. The album was meant to showcase both Beyoncé and her alter ego, Sasha Fierce. (An alter ego is a fictional, second identity that someone creates for themself, sometimes for performing.) She won five Grammys for the album and its singles.

Now that Beyoncé was married and had released her third solo album, she wanted to focus on other things. She was eager to learn more about the business side of music and also wanted to have children. She questioned if it would be possible to have a successful career and be a mother. But first, she needed to make a very difficult decision.

Mathew had been Beyoncé's manager almost as long as he'd been her father. He had taught Beyoncé everything she knew about hard work and fighting for what she deserved. But in 2011, Beyoncé discovered troubling news. Someone on her team said that Mathew was secretly taking money from her.

Beyoncé was heartbroken. She felt like she couldn't trust her father, so she hired someone to investigate whether or not he stole money from her. The investigators allegedly found proof that he had.

Beyoncé couldn't believe it. She could no longer have family managing her career. So, she made a difficult decision. She fired her father as her manager. Tina filed for divorce from Mathew shortly afterward. (Mathew and Tina had been having problems and living apart for a while.) This decision was difficult, but she had to do it.

Beyoncé with her mother and father

Beyoncé took a break from performing for nine months. She finally returned to the spotlight in June 2011 and released her fourth album. It was called *4*. Out of the seventy-two songs that she gave to Columbia Records, twelve were chosen. Many of the songs were influenced by

R&B from the 1970s and 1990s. "Party" (which featured rapper André 3000) and "Run the World (Girls)" became very popular. So did a song called "Love on Top."

In the summer of 2011, the MTV Video Music Awards took place in Los Angeles. Beyoncé and Jay arrived together. Though Beyoncé was excited to perform, she was also a little nervous. She was about to let the crowd in on a big secret.

André 3000

As Beyoncé walked onstage, she smiled at her fans. The first few notes of her hit song "Love on Top" began to play. Before she began singing, she said, "I want you to feel the love that's growing inside of me." As she sang, she didn't dance as energetically as she usually would.

As the song ended, the crowd went wild.
Beyoncé's smile was huge. She dropped her mic,
opened her sparkly purple tuxedo jacket, and

revealed her pregnant belly. Jay-Z was in the audience watching with pride. The secret was finally out—Beyoncé and Jay-Z were having a baby!

Beyoncé had a beautiful and healthy pregnancy. She felt very connected to her baby. On January 7, 2012, Blue Ivy Carter was born. (Carter is the last name of Jay-Z and Beyoncé's family.) Beyoncé immediately felt complete with her little girl.

CHAPTER 5
Secrets, Rumors, and Criticism

Throughout her career, Beyoncé became good at keeping secrets. It was important to her to have some things to herself. Whether it was about her art or personal life, Beyoncé wanted to control what people knew about her and how they found out.

On Friday, December 13, 2013, Beyoncé did something no artist had done before. At midnight, she released her fifth album, *Beyoncé*, with no warning. Fans were shocked! Usually, artists release single songs before an album. They share when their music is coming out beforehand and then

they try to get people excited to buy the album. New music was also usually released on Tuesdays, not Fridays. This release of the album on a Friday without warning changed the music industry forever.

Beyoncé was a special album. It strayed away from pop and returned to Beyoncé's R&B roots, this time with more complexity. There were songs featuring the people she loves the most, like Jay-Z and her daughter, Blue Ivy, who was almost two years old. The album had a song called "***Flawless" that included famous writer Chimamanda Ngozi Adichie speaking about the limitations placed on girls and women. Other popular songs were "Pretty Hurts" and "XO."

But what made the album even more special

Chimamanda Ngozi Adichie

was that it had a music video for every song! No one had ever seen such a production. Beyoncé received many awards for the project, including three Grammys. She became known not just as a singer or performer, but as an artist changing the music industry.

"Pretty Hurts" music video

However, Beyoncé soon learned that she couldn't control everything. On May 12, 2014, a private family matter became very public.

A video of an incident involving Beyoncé, Jay-Z, and her sister, Solange, went viral. It showed the group in a hotel elevator. A bodyguard tried to stop Solange from hitting Jay-Z but couldn't. An employee of the hotel sold the video to TMZ (a website known for sharing celebrity gossip), and soon the world knew about this private moment.

People wondered what the fight was about. Why didn't Beyoncé step in? Some people said that Solange was defending her sister. Rumors spread about Jay-Z having relationships with other women even though he was married to Beyoncé.

The family asked for privacy. But gossip would continue to spread.

That didn't stop Beyoncé. It made her more focused. Beyoncé and Jay-Z performed together in a worldwide tour called On the Run. They wanted to show everyone how good a team they were. Though the concert got rave reviews, some said it wasn't enough proof that their marriage was going well.

On the Run Tour

The attention on Beyoncé and Jay-Z wasn't only because of their relationship. Some people were less worried about their marriage and more concerned about how they were showing up for the Black community. The Black Lives Matter Movement had started, and many people  of all races were working together to bring attention to violence against Black people. But Beyoncé and Jay-Z had stayed quiet.

Many people were upset that Beyoncé and Jay-Z hadn't spoken up. Why weren't they using their music to address this important matter?

But they were doing their part. As protesters were getting arrested for standing up for what they believed in, Beyoncé and Jay-Z donated tens of thousands of dollars to bail people out of jail. They did this anonymously, meaning they kept it a secret. Some thought this wasn't enough. Beyoncé often used her music to address topics important to her. In her songs, she spoke about love and the hardships of marriage. She always sang about women's empowerment, so why not sing about Black empowerment?

Black Lives Matter (BLM)

In 2013, three Black women named Opal Tometi, Alicia Garza, and Patrisse Cullors started the Black Lives Matter movement. It began with a hashtag, #BlackLivesMatter, on social media after George Zimmerman was found not guilty for killing Trayvon Martin, a Black teenager. The movement grew in 2014 when Eric Garner and Michael Brown, two Black men, were killed by police officers. Many people were upset that the officers weren't charged for their crimes against these men, so protesters marched and chanted, "Black Lives Matter!"

Trayvon Martin

Social media helped more people learn about these events and see how unfairly Black people were being treated by the police, law enforcement, and other citizens. In 2020, the movement grew even more after Ahmaud Arbery was killed by two white men, who were not police officers, and George Floyd and Breonna Taylor were killed by police officers. Black Lives Matter continues to work hard for fair treatment, happiness, and safety for all Black people.

CHAPTER 6
Lemons and *Lemonade*

In February 2016, Beyoncé surprised her fans again. She released a song, along with a video, called "Formation." It had the familiar women's empowerment message that she'd been singing about since 1996 with Destiny's Child, but "Formation" also celebrated Black culture and Black empowerment. The video was inspired by New Orleans and featured various elements that celebrated Black culture. Black cowboys and Black people dancing in styles traditional to their cultures were featured. At the end of the video, there was a young boy with a hoodie and his hands up. This was meant to represent Trayvon Martin, who had been killed while wearing a hoodie. His birthday would've been the day before the song was released.

The day after "Formation" was released, Beyoncé performed at the Super Bowl. This wasn't her first show there. In 2013, she had been the main performer and reunited with Destiny's Child. This time, however, was a little different.

She wasn't the only performer: Coldplay was the headliner, and Bruno Mars and a few other performers were guests.

When it was time, Beyoncé marched onto the football field with a large group of women dressed in all-black and leather. They wore berets

modeled after the Black Panther Party, a political group from the 1960s and 1970s who fought for Black empowerment. Beyoncé was also wearing a black bodysuit and leather jacket that resembled an outfit once worn by Michael Jackson.

As the music started, Beyoncé said, "Okay ladies, now let's get in formation." As Beyoncé continued with the song, the women formed into the letter *X*. It was meant to represent Malcolm X, a famous Black activist known for his views that Black people should do whatever is necessary to protect their community. Some people did not agree with his beliefs.

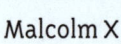

Malcolm X

Though Beyoncé was not the only performer that night, she made an impression on everyone. This was a different side of Beyoncé that no one had ever seen. Her performance was bold. It was political. While most reviews celebrated this new side of Beyoncé, there were many who criticized her. Some thought she was being *too* political with her performance. Some said she was antipolice for her support of the Black Lives Matter Movement. After the show, there was a plan to show up in front of the NFL's headquarters on February 16 to boycott Beyoncé. Almost no one showed up to protest against her, but there was a small crowd of people who came to *support* Beyoncé!

Beyoncé wasn't surprised that her performance sparked big reactions. She knew there were those who didn't want her to speak about the violence happening toward Black people. Some people didn't even want her to talk about her race at all. But at this moment, she knew that in order to be true to herself as an artist, a mother, and a Black woman, she needed to release this song.

She was always proud to be Black. And now, she was a mother to a little Black girl, who had already had racist things written and said about her. She felt it was her responsibility to use her art to speak her truth.

In an article, she said, "I hope I can create art that helps people heal. Art that makes people feel proud of their struggle. Everyone experiences pain, but sometimes you need to be uncomfortable to transform."

A few weeks after making that statement, Beyoncé released *Lemonade*. It was unlike anything she'd ever done before. This was not only an album; it was a movie.

Filmed in Louisiana, *Lemonade* celebrated Black history, Black community, and the love between Black people. Throughout most of the movie, Beyoncé was surrounded by Black women supporting her and caring for her. But the lyrics were mostly about a woman whose husband had betrayed her. People believed it was Beyoncé's way of sharing the truth about her marriage.

Throughout the album, she sings about the pain she has experienced. There's a song called "Daddy Lessons" that speaks to her complicated relationship with her father, but most of the other songs are about the challenges of her marriage.

But by the end of the film, we see that Beyoncé and Jay-Z have healed. She has forgiven him so that they can work on their family.

Almost at the album's end is a song called "Freedom." It features Kendrick Lamar and another special guest—Jay-Z's grandmother Hattie White. At the end of the song, she says, "I had my ups and downs, but I always find the inner strength to pull myself up. I was served lemons, but I made lemonade." Making lemons into lemonade is an old saying. It means to take something that is bitter or difficult and turn it into something sweet and nice through hard work and perseverance.

Kendrick Lamar

This is what Beyoncé did with her pain. She turned it into art that could help and empower other people.

Lemonade received many awards and even won a Peabody Award, one of the biggest honors given to artists.

In 2017, Beyoncé made another surprise announcement. This time she used her Instagram account. Under a photo of her kneeling in front of roses and holding her belly, Beyoncé wrote: "We would like to share our love and happiness. We have been blessed two times over. We are incredibly grateful that our family will be growing by two, and we thank you for your well wishes.—The Carters."

Beyoncé and Jay-Z were having twins! As Jay-Z expressed in his newly released song "4:44," this was a miracle he wanted to embrace.

Throughout their relationship, the couple had experienced difficult moments, but they had made lemons into lemonade. A new chapter was beginning.

CHAPTER 7
Coming Home

Shortly after announcing her pregnancy, Beyoncé had more news—she was headlining Coachella! A "headliner" is the main performer at a festival, and they are usually the final show of the day. Coachella is a big

Coachella

music festival in a desert in California. At the time, only one other woman had ever headlined the festival, Bjork. There had never been a Black woman headliner before. This was exciting news! Beyoncé had a plan for her performance.

Shortly after this announcement, however, she got advice from her doctors that she couldn't ignore. She needed to slow down. This pregnancy was more stressful than her last one. Beyoncé had to wait until after the babies were born to headline Coachella.

As the pregnancy continued, it only got more difficult. She had to stay in bed for a month before giving birth. The delivery of the babies was complicated, but Beyoncé gave birth to two healthy babies on June 13, 2017. They were named Rumi and Sir Carter. After giving birth, Beyoncé took some time to rest, but not for long. The next Coachella was coming up.

Beyoncé and her team rehearsed for four months. Hundreds of dancers and musicians were hired. This wasn't going to be an ordinary performance, this was going to be a homecoming! Beyoncé took the importance of her being the first Black woman as the main performer at the festival very seriously. She wanted her performance to celebrate Black culture. This included highlighting aspects of Historical Black Colleges and Universities (HBCUs).

HBCUs

There are over one hundred Historically Black Colleges and Universities (HBCUs) throughout the United States. Most HBCUs opened shortly after the Civil War. During this time, many universities didn't accept Black people. Those that did were often not welcoming places for Black students. Many colleges didn't accept Black students until after the Civil Rights Act of 1964. HBCUs have been spaces where Black students can further their studies while feeling safe and celebrated.

In addition to offering a strong education, HBCUs are known for their excellent marching bands. Many students even say that they chose their HBCU because of the reputation of the school's marching band. Marching bands at HBCUs have their own culture. They play classic songs but also new songs by popular Black musicians.

HBCUs have educated some of our nation's most brilliant and talented leaders, such as actor Chadwick Boseman, Vice President Kamala Harris, and Supreme Court Justice Thurgood Marshall. All attended Howard University, a famous HBCU. Dr. Martin Luther King Jr. received an honorary doctorate from Howard University.

Howard University

When Beyoncé shared with her mother that she was going to do an HBCU homecoming-themed performance, her mother wondered if this was a good idea. After all, Coachella drew a mostly white crowd. Would they understand traditions rooted in Black culture? Beyoncé felt that it was important to do what was best for the world rather than what was expected. She wanted to share her true voice.

HBCU homecoming performance

The show was called Beyoncé's Homecoming 2018. In true Beyoncé fashion, it was full of surprises. There were many elements highlighting Black culture, including a marching band that featured musicians from HBCUs. Beyoncé sang "Lift Ev'ry Voice and Sing"—often referred to as the national anthem for Black Americans. There were also dancers who did a step show, a tradition in Black sororities. (Sororities are organizations where women can come together to make new friends and form professional networks.)

She also had many guests performing with her, including Jay-Z and Solange. The biggest highlight was Michelle and Kelly performing with Beyoncé. Once again, Destiny's Child was back together. They sang classics, like "Say My Name" and "Soldier." Fans were happy to see them together again. The show was a huge success! It was streamed more than any other Coachella performance.

Beyoncé's Homecoming 2018, or "Beychella," as some called it, brought positive attention to HBCUs. More and more young people said they decided to apply to an HBCU after watching the show. After the performance, Beyoncé donated $100,000 to four HBCUs.

In 2019, a Netflix special called *Homecoming: A Film by Beyoncé* showed almost the entire concert. It also shared behind the scenes footage. In the documentary, Beyoncé shared what HBCUs meant to her. She said she always thought she would attend one

herself, but never got to because of her career.

In the film, Beyoncé also talked about her difficult pregnancy and the hard work to prepare for the concert. The documentary reminded the fans of Beyoncé's humanity *and* her exceptional talent. Most importantly, it showcased Black excellence. "Black excellence" is a phrase that describes how Black people have always been brilliant and innovative individuals, even as they faced extreme racism and adversity throughout history.

Just a few years before, people thought Beyoncé didn't speak about Black culture enough. Now, Beyoncé was using every moment she could to highlight the beauty and richness of Black culture.

CHAPTER 8
Mother, Africa

Beyoncé didn't have much time to rest after Coachella. In June, she needed to get on the road again. Her family joined her. The Carters—Beyoncé and Jay-Z—started the On the Run Tour II on June 6, 2018. Shortly after, they released their first album as a duo. It was called *Everything Is Love*. The successful tour ended at the Global Citizen Festival in South Africa. At every show, people had paid attention to Beyoncé's outfits. She wore bright colors and pieces of clothing traditional to African fashion. Beyoncé didn't only do this because she was in South Africa. She was hinting at her next projects.

In the summer of 2019, Disney released a

remake of the 1994 blockbuster *The Lion King*. Beyoncé played the adult version of the character Nala.

Beyoncé was excited to act again. Throughout her career, she had starred in several movies. *Dreamgirls* (2006) was one of the most successful, and it had won Academy Awards.

The pop star was especially excited to be in a movie for kids now that she had three children of her own.

Beyoncé produced an album to go with the hit movie called *The Lion King: The Gift*. It was a special soundtrack because it featured Afrobeats music. Afrobeats is a popular style of music originating from West Africa.

The producers of the album were from different parts of Africa. It featured popular Afrobeats singers like Mr Eazi, Tiwa Savage, Burna Boy, and Wizkid. Afrobeats music was

Wizkid

already popular, but this album would bring it to more people than ever before.

One of the album's most popular songs was called "Brown Skin Girl." It featured Beyoncé, SAINt JHN, Wizkid, and Blue Ivy, who was only seven years old when it was recorded! She is credited as a cowriter.

"Brown Skin Girl" celebrates the beauty of every shade of brown skin. This is important to both Beyoncé and Blue Ivy. Though Beyoncé has lighter skin, she's witnessed how colorism affects her community. Colorism is when people who have lighter skin are treated better than those with darker skin. The song and the music video reminded listeners that everyone is beautiful. The video featured dark-skinned women from many countries across the world.

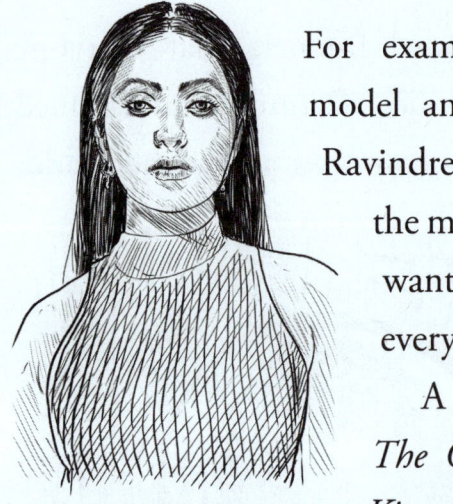

Sheerah Ravindren

For example, South Asian model and activist Sheerah Ravindren was featured in the music video. Beyoncé wanted to highlight everyone.

A visual album for *The Gift* called *Black Is King* was also released. Beyoncé used this film to highlight African culture and celebrate Black boys and men. Beyoncé said, "After having my son, Sir Carter, I felt it was important to uplift and praise our boys and to assure that they grow up with enough films, children's books, and music that promote

emotional intelligence, self-value, and our rich history. That's why the film is dedicated to him."

Beyoncé understood that she had the responsibility to make this film thoughtfully. Though she is of African descent, her ancestors have been in America for a long time. She needed to understand today's Africa if she was going to make a good film.

She hired African directors Emmanuel Adjei and Blitz Bazawule for the project. She worked with African fashion designers and hair stylists, too. She studied the music and culture of different African countries to make sure she was respectful. It took a lot of effort, but Beyoncé was proud of the final product.

Beyoncé's Films

Across documentaries and movies, Beyoncé has starred in over a dozen films. *Carmen: A Hip Hopera* (2001) was her first film and was shown on TV. *Austin Powers in Goldmember* (2002) was her first movie that played in theaters. She has starred in two animated films, *Epic* (2013) and *The Lion King* (2019).

Beyoncé in *Austin Powers in Goldmember*

CHAPTER 9
Beyoncé Is *Renaissance*

Beyoncé had been busy her whole life. Her days had been full of dancing, singing, and traveling. When the COVID-19 pandemic hit the world, it felt like time stopped for everyone—even Beyoncé. She could no longer tour or travel. But this didn't mean she stopped working.

How did she want to spend the next chapter of her career? She decided she would allow herself to focus on joy. During this time, she released a song called "Black Parade" on June 19—Juneteenth. (Juneteenth is a holiday celebrating the end of slavery in the United States. It remembers the day in 1865 when the last enslaved people in Texas were told they were free.) But this wasn't the only thing she was working on.

In 2022, Beyoncé announced a huge project. It would be released in three parts. First was an album of celebration that she created during the pandemic. It was called *Renaissance.* On her Instagram page, she shared why she created the album, calling it a place for her to dream and escape from the world during a scary time.

This album was also special because it was dedicated to someone Beyoncé loved very much, her Uncle Johnny. Uncle Johnny was actually Tina's nephew and Beyoncé's cousin, but he was much older than Beyoncé and was more like an uncle to her. He made her dresses and taught her about his favorite kind of music—house music. House music is very popular in the LGBTQIA+

community, and Uncle Johnny was gay. Sadly, Uncle Johnny died from an illness called acquired immunodeficiency syndrome (AIDS) when Beyoncé was seventeen. Though he was gone, his impact on Beyoncé would go on forever. This is why Beyonce dedicated the album to Uncle Johnny and the entire LGBTQIA+ community.

Uncle Johnny

"Break My Soul" was the first song released from the album *Renaissance*. It came out on June 20, 2022. The entire album was available the following month. The album was named the best album of the year by multiple media outlets and was nominated for nine Grammys. Beyoncé won four of those Grammys, making her the most awarded artist in

Grammy Awards history. However, *Renaissance* did not win Album of the Year. This was surprising because the album was celebrated by both critics and fans. Some saw this loss as racist and sexist.

When Beyoncé announced that she was taking *Renaissance* on a worldwide tour, fans went wild! People felt empowered by the album, and it changed their lives. Now, fans worldwide would

be able to experience *Renaissance* live. As soon as tickets were released, people spent hundreds of dollars on seats.

News articles were written about how the concert was helping the world's economy. Hotels in European cities had made tons of money from fans visiting new cities just to see Beyoncé. In Atlanta, the concert helped local businesses earn $10 million in revenue. Ticket sales for the tour broke worldwide records.

Kamala Harris

The concert was unlike anything ever seen before. There was even a suggested dress code for the concertgoers during Virgo season for Beyoncé's birthday: silver. Guests, including celebrities, spent days looking for the perfect silver outfit to wear. Even Vice President Kamala Harris showed up in a silver-sequined blouse.

Blue Ivy and Beyoncé

There were also special guests. As the tour traveled around the world, people tried to guess who Beyoncé was going to bring onstage with her. But the most special guest who performed with her was her older daughter, eleven-year-old Blue Ivy.

CHAPTER 10
Returning to Her Roots

In early 2024, Beyoncé headed to the Grammys to support Jay-Z, who was receiving the Dr. Dre Global Impact Award for his lifetime of success in music. At that point in his career, he had received twenty-four Grammys!

Jay-Z brought Blue up onstage with him when he accepted his award. He then gave an important speech. He shared his concern about the Grammys treating Black artists unfairly. He specifically pointed out that his wife, Beyoncé, had won the most Grammys ever but had never won Album of the Year. That seemed unfair to him and many others.

As Jay-Z spoke, everyone seemed to be looking at Beyoncé. Even before the speech, she had been drawing attention all night, especially in the fabulous cowboy hat she was wearing. Beyoncé was known for making fashion statements.

Even though she'd worn cowboy hats throughout her career, this look felt different. It was giving the audience a hint of Beyoncé's upcoming project.

Her next album—*Cowboy Carter*—would honor her Texas roots through country music.

When promoting the new album, Beyoncé shared on her Instagram page, "This album has been over five years in the making. It was born out of an experience that I had years ago where I did not feel welcomed . . . and it

was very clear that I wasn't. But, because of that experience, I did a deeper dive into the history of Country music and studied our rich musical archive."

Beyoncé was referring to the 2016 Country

Music Awards (CMAs). *Lemonade* had just been released. A song from the album, "Daddy Lessons," was the first time many people heard Beyoncé sing country. She was excited to sing with the Chicks, a country music group, at the CMAs.

Beyoncé and the Chicks

Unfortunately, not everyone was welcoming to Beyoncé. She was treated disrespectfully backstage, and audience members shouted terrible things at her during her performance. There were people who said Black people shouldn't sing country music and that they didn't belong in the industry. It was a crushing and confusing experience. Beyoncé was from the South . . . so were her parents. She had deep connections to country music. Why wasn't she allowed to sing country songs?

But, in true Beyoncé fashion, she used this experience as motivation. She wanted to learn more about her roots and the roots of country music. As she learned, she was reminded that Black people were always and still are a part of country music.

Beyoncé began *Cowboy Carter* during the pandemic. It was supposed to be act one for her three-act project. But she changed her mind. She felt that the pandemic had been so difficult that people deserved to dance, which is why she decided that *Renaissance* would be act one.

Beyoncé recorded around one hundred songs for the album. Only twenty-seven tracks were included.

On March 29, 2024, *Cowboy Carter* was available to the public. The album explored Beyoncé's southern roots, but all genres of music were included. Hip-hop, rock, country, and more were featured throughout the album. Famous country singers, like Dolly Parton, Willie Nelson, and Linda Martell, were also included in a number of songs. Martell was a trailblazer like Beyoncé, and she is considered by many to be the most successful Black woman artist in country music.

Linda Martell

Black Country Music

Black people have been a part of country music for over a century. In the 1920s, Deford Bailey was the first Black star to be a part of the Grand Ole Opry. This is a popular country radio show known for live country music. Bailey was known for playing his harmonica, and everyone loved it.

Deford Bailey

Linda Martell from South Carolina was the first Black woman to perform at the Grand Ole Opry. She started her career as an R&B singer but turned to country music in the late 1960s. In the 1960s and 1970s, Charley Pride became the first Black country superstar. In the 1980s and 1990s, Cleve Francis from Louisiana, a doctor, also pursued a country music career to much acclaim. Darius Rucker from the rock group Hootie and the Blowfish had almost a dozen top ten country hits as a solo artist.

Though Black people have always been a part of country music, it hasn't been easy for them to get the attention they deserve. Due to racism, it can be rare for country radio stations to play Black musicians, and it has been even harder for Black women.

Beyoncé also used her album to promote lesser-known Black country artists, including Tanner Adell, Brittney Spencer, Tiera Kennedy, Reyna Roberts, and Shaboozey. Including Black artists on the album brought more attention to people who were often ignored in country music.

Overall, people loved the album. Beyoncé was the first Black woman to be at the top of Billboard Top Country Albums chart. Though many loved her album, there were still people saying that Beyoncé should stay away from country music.

On February 2, 2025, Beyoncé attended the Grammy Awards. Though this award show had often disappointed Beyoncé, this time was different. She became the first Black woman to win the Grammy Award for Best Country Album. Then, something even better happened: Beyoncé finally won the Grammy for Album of the Year. In doing so, she became the fourth Black woman in history to win the award.

Beyoncé has been entertaining the world and breaking barriers most of her life. Each time she reaches a goal, she creates a new one for herself. And just when you think she's done it all, she figures out how to outshine herself and bring others along with her.

No matter what Beyoncé creates next, it will surely be just as thoughtful, groundbreaking, and entertaining as she is.

Timeline of Beyoncé's Life

1981	Beyoncé Giselle Knowles is born in Houston, Texas
1990	Joins girl group called Girl's Tyme
1992	Performs on TV competition *Star Search* with Girl's Tyme and loses
1996	Forms Destiny's Child with Kelly Rowland, LeToya Luckett, and LaTavia Roberson
1997	Destiny's Child signs with Columbia Records
1999	Releases *The Writing's on the Wall* as part of Destiny's Child
2003	Releases first solo album, *Dangerously in Love*
2005	Announces Destiny's Child is ending
2008	Marries Jay-Z
2012	Gives birth to Blue Ivy on January 6
2013	Releases first visual album, *Beyoncé*, without advance notice
2017	Gives birth to twins, Rumi and Sir Carter, on June 13
2018	Headlines Coachella, the first Black woman to do so
2020	Releases her third visual album, *Black Is King*
2022	Releases album *Renaissance*
2024	Releases album *Cowboy Carter*
2025	*Cowboy Carter* wins Album of the Year at the Grammy Awards

Timeline of the World

1981	Antigua and Barbuda gain independence from Britain
1983	Michael Jackson does the moonwalk for the first time in front of an audience
1989	World Wide Web is invented by English computer scientist Tim Berners-Lee
1991	Rodney King is filmed being attacked by police
1994	Apartheid ends in South Africa with first-ever democratic election in the country
2003	US military invades Iraq
2008	President Barack Obama is elected the first Black president
2009	Sonia Sotomayor becomes the first Latina woman to serve on the Supreme Court of the United States
2010	Instagram is founded by Kevin Systrom
2013	#BlackLivesMatter is tweeted for the first time
2015	Same-sex marriage is made legal by the US Supreme Court
2020	COVID-19 spreads globally
	Protests for racial equality take place worldwide
2021	Juneteenth becomes a federal holiday
2024	Summer Olympics take place in Paris

Bibliography

*Books for young readers

*Lavette, Lavaille, and Anastasia Williams. *Beyoncé: A Little Golden Book Biography*. New York: Golden Books, 2023.

*Sanchez Vegara, Maria Isabel, and Jade Orlando. *Little People, Big Dreams: Beyoncé*. Beverly, MA: Frances Lincoln Children's Books, 2024.

*Wilkins, Ebony Joy. *Trailblazers: Beyoncé: Queen of the Spotlight*. New York: Random House Books for Young Readers, 2020.